Rogue Animals

Althea Brooks
Illustrated by Liz Wilks

Alfred Collins was just nine years old
when his father was savagely
attacked by a wild boar.
It was 1984 and they were working
on the family property near Marlborough,
Central Queensland, Australia.
This is his story of bravery and courage.

TRUE STORIES
OF BRAVERY & COURAGE

BRAVE KIDS

BlueCatBooks

First published in 2004
BlueCatBooks
PO Box 3006
Eltham VIC 3095
Australia

email: peguero@bigpond.net.au
website: www.bluecatbooks.com.au

Text © Althea Brooks, 2004
Illustrations © Liz Wilks, 2004

National Library of Australia
Cataloguing-in-Publication entry:

Brooks, Althea.
 Rogue animals: true stories of bravery and courage.

 For children aged 8+.
 ISBN 0 9578422 7 9.

 1. Dangerous animals - Juvenile literature. 2. Heroes - Juvenile literature. 3. Courage - Juvenile literature. I. Wilks, Liz. II. Title. (Series : Brave kids ; book two).

 179.6

All rights reserved. Except under the conditions described in the Copyright Act 1968 of Australia and subsequent amendments, no part of this publication may be reproduced, stored in a retrieval system, or transmitted in any form or by any means, electronic or mechanical, photocopying, recording, or any information storage and retrieval system without written permission from the publisher.

Book & cover design by Lee Lewis
Printed in Australia by McPherson's Printing Group

Distributed nationally and in New Zealand
by Dennis Jones & Associates

WHAT WOULD YOU DO?

A raging boar is savaging your dad.
A large crocodile is attacking your friend.
You and your friends have drifted a long way
from land in rough seas.

How can any of us be sure what we would do
if faced with such dilemmas?

We do know, however, that the children in these
stories decided to place themselves
in just that kind of danger to save someone
else's life.

**Each of the stories in the BRAVE KIDS
series is based on a true incident of bravery.
While some details have been
added, the basic stories have been
confirmed from available records.**

Acknowledgements

Thanks are due to the Royal Humane Society of Australasia for allowing us to use a representation of the Clarke Gold Medal and for kindly providing relevant information.

Please note: Unless otherwise specified, awards indicated are from the Royal Humane Society of Australasia.

Contents

1	Alfie's Plan	9
2	On the Farm	12
3	The Hunt	16
4	Wild Pig Tracks	20
5	At the Truck	23
6	Lying in Wait	26
7	Charge!	29
8	Tusks & Teeth	32
9	Save Me!	35
10	Alfie's Promise	38
11	Help at Last	41
12	Just in Time	44
	Bravery Awards	46
	Alfie's Award	47

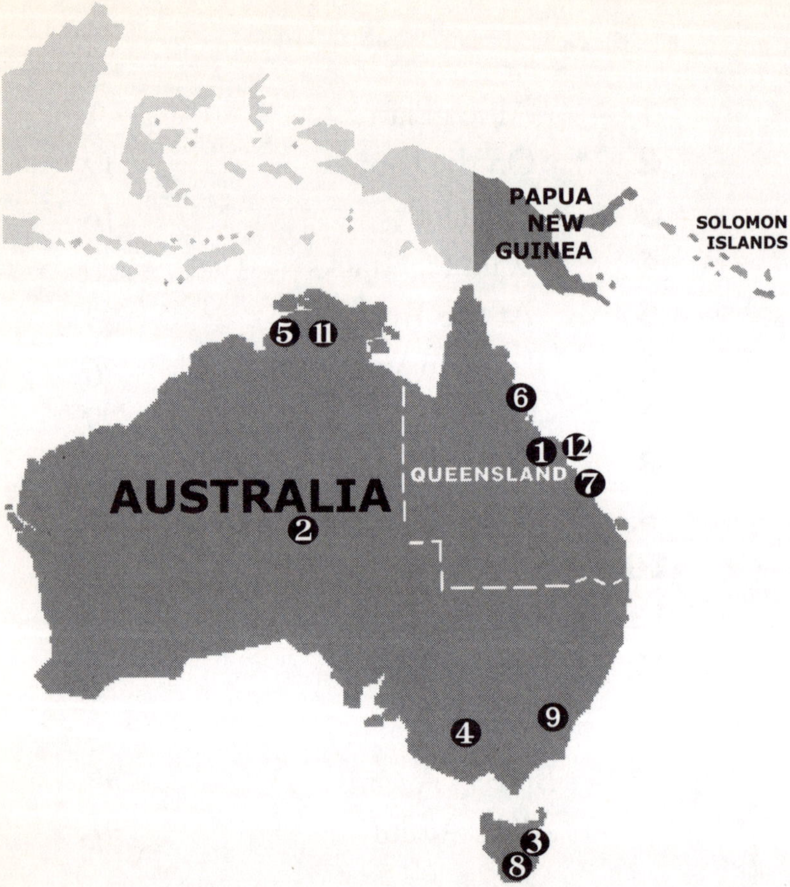

PAPUA NEW GUINEA

SOLOMON ISLANDS

AUSTRALIA

QUEENSLAND

6

MAP KEY
For location of rogue animal incidents

1 Marlborough, QLD
2 Uluru, NT
3 Campbell Town, TAS
4 Amphitheatre, VIC
5 Sweets Lookout, NT
6 Cairns, QLD
7 Fraser Island, QLD
8 Huon, TAS
9 Canberra, ACT
10 Dunedin, New Zealand
11 Nitmiluk National Park, NT
12 Rockhampton, QLD

FIJI

NEW ZEALAND

BOOK ICON KEY

 Topic information

 *Rogue animal incident*

Wild pigs can be found in many parts of Australia. Generally, it is thought that they descended from European pigs that escaped during settlement. But Aboriginal paintings depict wild pigs that look like the Asian variety. So it is possible that pigs were also brought across by Islander trading parties.

At the time of this story few wild pigs had been seen in the Marlborough district, Central Queensland, Australia, where the events of this story take place.

 # Alfie's Plan

Alfie Collins stopped writing and looked out the window. His dad was heading off in the truck to work on some fencing. He wished he could go too.

The Collins family lived on a beef-raising property near Marlborough. The closest school was too far away for him to go each day so Alfie did his school lessons at home.

Sometimes he wondered what it would be like to

go to school with other kids his age. But mostly he felt lucky to live on a farm.

His dad had agreed he could help out the next day, as long as he had finished his school work.

Wild pigs

Wild pigs (also known as wild boars or feral pigs) can be found in various parts of the world including America, Europe and Outback Australia. Most of those in Australia are originally descended from domestic pigs (**Sus scrofa**) introduced from Europe during early settlement. At that time they often roamed freely, scrounging for food in the bush. Inevitably some turned feral—living and breeding in the wild.

Wild pigs come in many different colours, shapes and sizes. They look similar to domestic farm pigs, but are usually covered in coarse hair and have longer snouts.

Adult feral pigs grow a protective shield of cartilage under the skin of the shoulders to help protect their ribs when fighting. Because of their appearance, they have been called **razorbacks**.

Adult male pigs weigh up to 200 kilos. Female wild pigs are roughly one-third smaller than the males, and do not have tusks.

So that was what he planned to do. He put his head down and worked hard. 'I'll make sure I finish today,' he decided.

Domestic pigs

Domestic pigs have short tails, hooved feet, small eyes, and a flat snout used to dig for food.

They are highly intelligent animals with a large vocabulary of sounds, and are often thought to be cleverer than dogs.

In the right conditions, domestic pigs can be kept as pets. They are known for being as loyal to their owners as dogs.

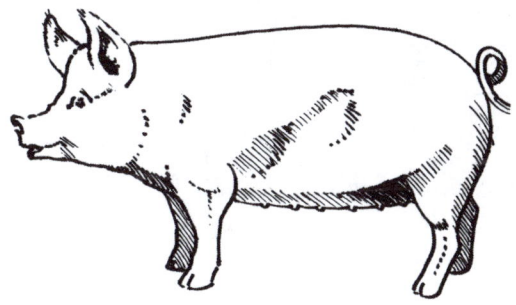

Both wild and domestic pigs belong to the group of animals known as **mammals**, which means they:
- are warm-blooded
- nourish their young with milk from the mother
- grow hair on their body.

The adult female pig is called a **sow**.
The adult male pig is called a **boar**.
A group of pigs is called a **sounder**.

The saying to 'sweat like a pig' is inaccurate, as pigs cannot sweat. Instead, they wallow in mud to protect their fair skin from the sun and to keep cool.

On the Farm

As he drove across the property, Alfie's dad saw something move in the distance. He stopped and jumped out of the truck to get a closer look.

He could just make out the shape of a huge, black boar. Its snout was digging in the soil.

Just yesterday he had finished a grading job in that spot, which had levelled out the soil. Now the pig was rooting up all his hard work.

'Wild pig,' he muttered. 'I hope there aren't any more of those around!'

As he drove on, he remembered that a cow had died recently and that its carcass was lying in the grass nearby.

That was probably what had attracted the wild pig to the area, he realised. He had never seen one on the property before.

The Collins family were sitting down to dinner later that evening when he told them about it.

'We've got an urgent job to do tomorrow.'

'What is it, Dad?' asked Alfie eagerly.

'I saw a wild boar this afternoon,' his dad replied. Everyone looked up, surprised.

Alfie was excited. He had never seen a wild boar, though he had heard about them. 'So what do we do, Dad?'

'We'll check to see if it's still around that dead cow,' his dad said.

'What if it is?' asked the oldest of Alfie's three sisters.

No-one said anything, but their dad looked grim.

 Wild pigs often cause soil damage by digging, which destroys vegetation that native and domesticated animals depend on for food. Digging also reduces the groundcover which allows weeds to invade.
　They also kill and eat newborn lambs, which may not always be noticed as they usually eat the entire carcass.

Pig in the Parsley

24 July 1999

Wild pigs in Outback Australia have been a pest for many years. And it's not only the farmers who are troubled by them.

Nicole Watson, a resident of north Queensland, was warned by a friend about wild pigs in the area.

'I just put it out of my mind,' Nicole said recently, 'then I was picking parsley in my yard and I saw a black hairy beast about ten metres away. It was a bit bigger than a medium-sized dog and it had incredible tusks.'

Not surprisingly, she was unsure what to do.

'We just stared at each other,' Nicole added. 'Then it turned and wandered off.'

That was when she contacted the Department of Natural Resources, Mines and Energy. They promptly sent a qualified hunter to trap the animal.

The department representative said that there are four commonly-used techniques of control: hunting, trapping, poisoning and fencing.

In the tropics, hunting with dogs had been a favoured method. But now, the trap design is improved and can capture many wild pigs at one time.

The use of poison is also successful, except that there is no 'pig-specific' bait available.

To maintain a small area, fencing is the most effective method, but can be expensive.

'I don't suppose it is likely to happen often,' said Nicole, 'but if it does contact your local government department.'

'Traps now have a trigger that only pigs can open,' explained a representative of the department. 'This avoids trapping native animals, like wallabies; or endangered species, such as cassowaries. Traps need to be set every night and checked each day.'

While feral pigs are a declared pest, it is expected that hunters remove them from traps humanely and without delay.

Meantime, let's hope that Nicole doesn't meet any more pigs in the parsley at the bottom of her garden.

3 The Hunt

The following morning Alfie and his dad got into the truck with all three of his young sisters, who were keen to come too.

The youngest asked, 'Where will we look for the boar, Dad?'

'You won't be looking for it at all. You and your sisters have to stay in the truck.'

'Why, Dad? Are wild pigs dangerous?'

'Yes, darling. Any wild animal can turn aggressive and be very dangerous to humans. There are stories of attacks by buffaloes, dingoes, and even kangaroos.'

The Story of Azaria

In the winter of 1980, the Chamberlain family went camping at Uluru, in Central Australia.

On the evening of 17 August, nine-week-old baby Azaria Chamberlain went missing from the family tent. Her mother, Lindy Chamberlain, ran to tell the other campers that a dingo had taken the baby.

Only weeks before, there had been official reports of dingo attacks on children, and on the night Azaria disappeared,

dingoes were seen close to the camping area.

Witnesses nearby heard a growl just before Lindy discovered her baby missing, and there were dingo tracks found leading away from the tent. Blood was also found on the inside of the tent.

Azaria's body was never found, although her blood-soaked clothing was discovered a week after her disappearance.

In 1982, Lindy Chamberlain was found guilty of murdering her daughter. Her husband, Michael Chamberlain, was convicted as an accessary to the crime.

The evidence used to convict the Chamberlains was later found to be questionable. In 1986, Azaria's matinee jacket was also discovered and Lindy was finally released from prison. In 1988, the Chamberlains were found to be innocent of any crime.

This was perhaps the most well-known animal attack the world had ever seen.

No wonder Alfie's dad had brought a rifle along. But it wasn't loaded. 'Best not to take risks,' he always said.

They were going to start looking for the boar in the area where the dead cow lay.

'Will you have to shoot it, Dad?' asked Alfie.

'Can't we just scare it off?'

'Well, they dig up crops, knock over fencing, foul up water supplies and kill small animals, even newborn lambs.'

'Then why can't they all be killed if they're so bad?' the oldest daughter asked.

Alfred Collins smiled. 'For a start, there's tens of thousands of them in the Outback.'

Bizarre Boar Behaviour

Wild boars are still to be found in Europe. As their habitat is being destroyed they are often forced into close contact with humans in their search for food. For example:

- Imagine the staff's surprise at a hotel in one of Romania's Black Sea resorts, when a hairy and tusked visitor weighing at least 100 kg tried to check in. Witnesses were said to be so scared they considered checking out! Instead the boar, in turn scared by the startled hotel guests, crashed through a window and escaped, leaving a trail of blood and broken glass.

- A man in Britain, who surprised a boar in woodlands, spent many hours up a tree waiting for it to leave the area.

- French farmers have complained about wild boars constantly digging up valuable truffles.

'Have you ever eaten one?' said Alfie's oldest sister.

'No, we're not allowed to sell the meat here in Australia, because of the diseases that it might carry,' said their dad.

As they drove along the track, Alfie was starting to feel a little nervous. He wondered how he would feel if they really did come across a wild boar.

Bizarre Boar Behaviour

- Perhaps most surprising of all, in Berlin, a rampaging wild boar disturbed an elderly German couple's afternoon nap. It broke into their ground-floor apartment, and leapt into bed with them, before biting the man and fleeing.

  Neighbours told police the boar crashed through the glass front door of the apartment building and then rammed open the door to the couple's apartment. After a thorough search, no trace could be found of the invading boar, apart from a trail of blood.

  The 71-year-old man was not badly hurt.

- In December 2003 in Spain, a wild boar's two-day sea swim only ended when police hauled the creature to shore off the Costa Brava coast. At first the police had thought it to be a swimmer in distress and launched a rescue. Later, it was guessed that the boar had fallen into a current at the water's edge after days of heavy rain and drifted out to sea.

 # Wild Pig Tracks

The Collins' property was certainly big. It took almost twenty minutes to drive to where Alfie's dad had seen the dead cow. Then it was time to get to work.

 Pigs are **omnivores**. This means that, like humans, they eat both meat and plants. Generally, they rely on plant material for the main part of their diet. They also eat anything from insects to small mammals.

Wild pigs can carry diseases that may harm humans and livestock. Foot and mouth disease, tuberculosis, anthrax and tapeworm parasites are just a few examples of the germs they may carry.

Alfie and his dad jumped out of the truck. The younger children knew they had to stay put.

The carcass was about a hundred metres away through thick scrub.

Alfie's dad stopped to point out where the boar had rooted up the soil the previous day.

'That's how you can tell if there's been a wild pig around,' he explained.

They made their way over to the carcass. As expected, the cow had been torn apart. Alfie gaped at all the blood and remains. They looked around, but there were no signs of a boar.

Phillipa Mary O'Brien was only nine years of age when she was awarded the Clarke Bronze Medal and the Rupert Wilks Trophy in 1957.

In Campbell Town, Tasmania, a steer became angry and separated from its herd at the slaughter house. It charged toward the road where Phillipa and her young brother, James, were walking.

As it approached, Phillipa tried to lift James to safety over a fence, but she couldn't do it. So bravely, she placed him on the ground and stood over him as the animal ran towards them. The steer knocked her over as it passed and kept running down the road. Fortunately, neither of the the children was hurt.

 # At the Truck

Alfie's sisters waited back at the truck as their dad had said. But after a while, they started to feel anxious.

'I wonder if there's more than one wild pig around. Dad said there were lots of them, didn't he.'

 Billy Corcoran of Amphitheatre, Victoria, was only nine years of age when he received a bravery award for the rescue of his father from a bull attack on 22 August 1994.
Around 4.30 pm Billy's father was drafting some cattle in a neighbour's yard when a steer rammed a gate behind him. The gate then struck Mr Corcoran in the back and he fell, losing all feeling in his legs. A young bull then charged and forced him up against the gate. As the bull began to gore his father, Billy ran into the yard with a piece of timber. He attacked the bull repeatedly about the head, until it was forced away.
Billy then phoned for assistance and waited with his father until help arrived.

'"Thousands", he said.'

'No, he said "tens of thousands"!'

Their imaginations started to run wild.

'What if one came along right now? Could it get in the truck?'

The oldest sister tried to reassure them. 'We're safe here. Dad said to stay put until they get back and we'll be okay.'

But the questions made her start to worry too. I hope we'll be all right. I wish they'd hurry back, she thought to herself.

Very few wild animals turn rogue. Many of them simply live out their daily lives, hunting for food, and sleeping.

But a small number of animals become angry or frightened when confronted by humans.

One such animal was Sweetheart, a massive crocodile from the Finniss River near Darwin (see **Brave Kids**, Book One, *Crocodile Attack*). Sweetheart was known for tackling boats—unusual behaviour for crocodiles.

The first attack was in 1974 at Sweets Lookout Billabong. Three people were fishing from a boat at night when the crocodile surfaced, grabbed the boat and shook it violently.

Despite several such attacks, no-one was injured.

Marlie Coleman of Cairns, Queensland, became the first female to receive the RSPCA Australia Humane Award. This award is given to those who have shown courage by risking their personal safety to rescue an animal.

Five years old at the time, Marlie was playing with her kitten, Sooty, in her backyard. It was there that a scrub python attacked and wrapped its jaws around the kitten. Immediately, Marlie went to rescue her pet. The sharp-toothed python let go of the kitten, but then struck at the girl, attaching itself to her lip.

Marlie's mother heard her screams and ran into the backyard to find her daughter standing on the barbecue with a snake attached to her face. She was bleeding and sobbing that the snake was trying to eat Sooty. Her mother pulled the python off and it disappeared. On the way to the hospital, Marlie's only concern was for her kitten.

The RSPCA acknowledged her selfless and courageous act, but said that the organisation does not want to see children place themselves in danger.

While Sooty, the kitten, was only slightly injured, Marlie still has scars from the horrific attack.

Scrub pythons grow to around three metres long. They are non-venomous, but are known for defending themselves by biting with their long, sharp teeth. Their prey usually includes small mammals such as chickens, small cats and dogs.

6 Lying in Wait

Alfie's dad was standing over the carcass, trying to work out how the cow had died. He didn't notice the two beady eyes staring at them, or the slight movement in the long grass.

The wild boar was lying in wait.

Animal instinct told it that these intruders were a threat to its food . . . to its survival.

Meanwhile, Alfie was busy asking his dad questions about the cow, and whether the boar would come back.

'There's not much we can do now,' his father replied. 'We may have to set some traps.'

Alfie hoped he'd be allowed to help.

'We'd better head back,' his dad added. 'The girls will be wondering where we are.'

Kangaroos usually keep to themselves and rogue attacks are uncommon. However, on holiday in Queensland, John Crouch was standing outside his caravan when a two-metre-high kangaroo pounced on him. The animal then turned to John's wife, Helen, and began scratching her face, back and stomach. John was forced to destroy the animal before it could kill her. He suffered a badly sprained hand, scratches and bruising.

Wildlife officers believe the animal may have been a pet that had been released or had escaped. This could explain why a usually calm animal had become enraged without being provoked.

In 2001, the Gage family was holidaying on Fraser Island, off the coast of Queensland, which is home to large numbers of dingoes.

Ross Gage took his seven-year-old son, Dylan, to look for his older brother, Clinton, who had gone to play with a friend on the sand dunes.

Ahead, Ross saw a body, mauled and dead. With horror, he recognised it as his son. Then he heard screams from behind him, and turned to find Dylan being attacked too. Ross went to his younger son's aid, and then the dingo turned on him. He picked up Dylan, and went back to Clinton's body where the dingo had returned and was still attacking the dead boy.

The father picked both boys up, and was followed by the dingo back to their tent.

It is believed that the dingoes actually stalked the nine-year-old and his friend, who had been able to escape.

The Gage family had not seen any dingoes beforehand, but they were aware of the many recent dingo attacks on the island.

Later, a male and female dingo were destroyed.

The boy's death started a public appeal that dingoes on the island be culled, that is, to be reduced in numbers.

Dogs can make wonderful and loving pets, but sadly, some dogs have also been responsible for attacking humans.

If dogs are treated with kindness and respect, it is most unlikely that they will attack a human. Responsible owners should have voice control of their pets and always supervise them around children. Dog obedience school is an excellent way to train and socialise an animal, and is fun for both the dog and owner.

 # Charge!

Alfie and his dad turned to leave the area where they had found the pig diggings. Then, with little more than a rustle, the boar charged.

From its hiding place close by, it reached them in just a few seconds. Standing a few steps away from

his dad, Alfie screamed and dived for cover as the massive boar slammed into his father.

It crashed into him with such force, he was knocked straight to the ground. The animal must have weighed at least 120 kilos, maybe more.

The rifle fell just out of reach. In any case, it still wasn't loaded.

Young Alfie watched in horror.

A bull is likely to show aggression when it thinks its dominance is being challenged.

Bull calves raised in groups are less likely to attack people than bull calves raised alone in their own pens. When they grow up with their own kind, they know that they are cattle and not human. As adult bulls, they are then less likely to think that people are part of the herd.

When bulls are young it is important that people don't play butting games with them. It may seem fun at the time, but when they grow up it may prove dangerous. If supervised, it is okay to stroke calves under the chin, on the rear or shoulders, but never the forehead.

On 23 September 1962, in Huon, Tasmania, 12-year-old Gregory Hassell was sitting on a fence when he witnessed a bull attack. Albert Bennett, his neighbour, had been feeding his Friesian bull. Without warning, the bull knocked him to the ground and repeatedly butted him with its sharp horns.

Immediately, Gregory jumped down, grabbed a stick and began to strike the bull on the face as hard as he could. This distracted the bull and it turned away from Albert, who managed to climb out of the paddock.

Gregory Hassell was awarded the Clarke Bronze Medal, and the Rupert Wilks Trophy in 1963.

 # 8 Tusks & Teeth

Alfie's dad tried to fight back against the deadly attacker. He kicked furiously, aiming for the head, but it was as if the boar's entire body was covered in armour.

Then the pig ripped into his left boot. It sliced through the leather with its tusks and teeth, savaging his feet.

Then it bit at his legs, tore away the muscle of his right calf and gouged out bone. Blood spurted from the wound.

Snarling and snapping, the wild boar attacked him

again. Alfred Collins could see it was the end, if he didn't act quickly. He gathered every last bit of strength and grabbed the pig by its tusks. But the beast was too strong. It shook him free and sank its teeth into his hand.

He could no longer fight.

Magpies have a reputation for protecting their nests. They may attempt to peck and scratch at the head unless they are being directly looked at. Many people, who are aware of magpies in their local area, wear ice-cream containers with pretend eyes stuck on the top to ward off any attacks.

In the year 2000, the magpie problem started to get out of control in Canberra, the capital city of Australia. Angry magpies, sometimes twenty or more, began swooping on passers-by during the breeding season. They particularly targeted women with red hair, cyclists and mothers with prams, though nobody is sure why. There were 254 recorded attacks during that mating season.

These magpies even made an appearance at the Sydney Olympics that year, swooping on a group of mountain-bike riders.

The residents of Canberra took to wearing hard hats and using open umbrellas or sticks with streamers to protect themselves.

Kambo
In Papua New Guinea, pig tusks are known as 'kambo', which literally means treasures. These are traditionally made into ornaments or jewellery.

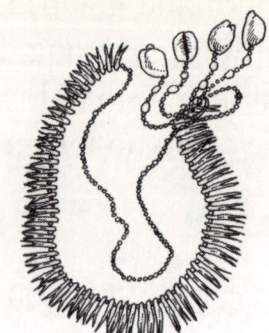

Kambo pono
A necklace of pig tusks is called 'kambo pono'.

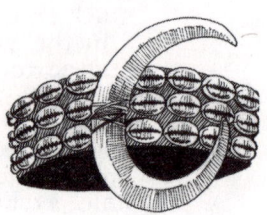

Beo kambo
A headband is called 'beo kambo' and worn as a bravery award from the village people.

Pig tusks have also been worn through the nose, and used as a traditional form of money.

 # 9 Save Me!

Blood gushed from his wounds as Alfie's dad cried out, 'Save me, Alf! Save me!'

From the nearby scrub, Alfie felt helpless as he watched the terrible attack on his father. It was all happening so fast, there seemed to be nothing he could do.

The boar was almost a metre in height. Surely his own 28 kilos wasn't enough to tackle such an animal.

But when Alfie heard his father's cries for help, he made his decision. He grabbed the biggest branch

he could find, and ran at the boar hitting its body wherever he could.

At first the shouting and whacking distracted the animal.

Briefly, it stopped its attack. Alfie's dad tried to move while he had the chance, but he was too badly wounded.

Angered, the boar turned to start its attack all over again. But Alfie would not give up. Desperately, he tried to stand over his dad to keep the boar from causing more damage. Again and again he struck at it.

But would his efforts be enough to frighten off the enraged boar? He was only a small boy up against a strong and heavy animal.

Wild pigs were introduced to New Zealand by Captain Cook and other explorers in the 1770s to be used as a food source by the early settlers. They are often referred to as 'Captain Cookers'.

Many wild pigs today are a mix of several domestic breeds that escaped from farms and adapted to the wild. They live in a variety of habitats, from alpine country to lowland forests.

[ROGUE] At first the cassowary may seem an unlikely rogue animal. However, over the year there have been reports of attacks on hikers. Also, in 2001, a San Francisco Zoo reported that an employee had been injured by a cassowary. It had torn into his leg with its powerful claws.

Cassowaries are large, flightless birds, related to the ostrich, emu and rhea. They are very territorial, so it is dangerous to go near the males in their cages. They can grow almost two metres in height and have dagger-like claws. Although they cannot fly, they can defend themselves with powerful kicks when threatened.

[ROGUE] A police spokesman in Dunedin, New Zealand, reported an incident where a runaway ewe ran into a garage and attacked one of the constables who had followed it. He said it could be facing charges of assaulting a police officer and unlawfully entering a building!

The officer concerned had suffered ripped trousers and bruising after being butted. The officer's colleague had thrown the sheep to the ground and handcuffed a front leg to a back leg. Unfortunately, the keys to the handcuffs later went missing, and back-up help was needed.

Fortunately, the officers had maintained a sense of humour about the incident concerning this most unlikely rogue beast.

10 Alfie's Promise

Alfie kept hitting the boar, even though he was exhausted. Then, at last, it turned and ran off into the scrub.

Alfie was relieved to see it finally go, but he couldn't rest yet.

He realised just how badly his father was hurt. Blood was everywhere.

'C'mon, Dad! Wake up!'

He placed his hands behind his father's back and helped him to sit up.

'It's okay, Dad. We have to get back to the truck. I'll help you up.' Alfie summoned all his strength and hauled his dad up by the waist.

'Lean on me,' he said, as they struggled the hundred metres or so back towards the truck.

His dad had lost so much blood that his face was pale, and every bit of him shook. 'It's all right, Dad. We'll make it,' Alfie promised.

He dragged his dad, barely conscious, and helped him up into the cabin of the truck.

Alfie shut the door and jumped into the driver's side.

His young sisters were shocked and scared when they saw their dad's injuries.

Alfie looked at the keys in the ignition, took a deep breath, stepped on the clutch and started the truck.

'But you can't drive!' one of his sisters shrieked. 'It's okay,' he said, 'I know what to do.'

He looked over at his dad and saw he'd lost consciousness again. He would have to do this on his own. With his father losing so much blood there was no time to waste.

How he wished he had paid better attention when his parents were driving. It was going to be a bumpy ride but at least they were moving.

It wasn't going to be easy, but somehow he would make it.

A group of 16 tourists was trekking in the Nitmiluk National Park in the Northern Territory of Australia when a 750-kilo buffalo bull charged without warning. Most of the tourists fled, hiding in nearby scrub. Two British tourists, a teenage boy and girl, were knocked over before the animal was scared away by others in the group.

Because old rogue buffaloes usually don't have good eyesight, the people in the scrub were safe. The two injured tourists were taken to Katherine Hospital. The girl had minor injuries and the boy required x-rays to check his spine.

The buffalo was found and destroyed by a park ranger. There are very few water buffaloes left in the park. Most of them have been shot for disease control purposes.

 # Help at Last

It was quite a few kilometres to the homestead. But at last Alfie had done it—he had driven the truck all the way home. And his dad was still alive.

'Quick, run and get Mum!' Alfie shouted as he sounded the horn in warning. His sisters jumped out and ran inside. Their mum came rushing out when she heard the noise.

Seeing how badly hurt her husband was, she ran back inside the house and returned with an armful of towels and a first aid kit.

The towels were wrapped around the wounds that

were bleeding the most. 'Alfie, press down here,' she said. 'We have to stop the bleeding.'

When she had done all she could, Mrs Collins got into the driver's seat.

She called out to her oldest daughter. 'Take your sisters inside and look after them. I'll ask a neighbour to come over.'

The girls were still very frightened. They hoped their dad would be all right.

'It's going to be okay. We're going to the Rockhampton Hospital. I'll telephone you when we get there,' Mrs Collins called to her daughters, as she drove away.

Alfie sat between his mum and dad in the truck. He was relieved that he didn't have to drive anymore. They were going all the way to Rockhampton. It was the nearest hospital to Marlborough, but it was 130 kilometres away. That meant it would take two hours or more to get there.

He looked at his dad who had his eyes closed and hoped he wasn't in too much pain.

Alfie could see that his mum was really worried.

She was frowning and her jaw was clenched.

His dad's pulse was faint, but still there. 'Please let him be okay,' he thought.

Rogue animals may not necessarily live in the wild. In 2001, at the London Zoo, a zoo-keeper was crushed to death by a 20-year-old female elephant weighing four tonnes.

The keeper, James Robson, was going about his duties when the elephant pinned him down and stamped on his head. The shocked visitors, who witnessed the attack, said it appeared to be deliberate.

The man screamed for help, but could not escape. The zoo claimed that he was following safety procedures, and that Mr Robson was an experienced handler.

A wildlife group, commenting on the incident, said that the elephant was living in cramped conditions and had previously been showing signs of distress. One elephant in the enclosure had even been seen shaking its head for twenty minutes.

 # 12 Just in Time

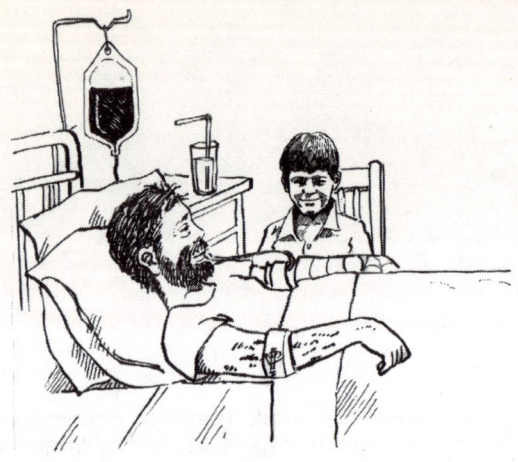

Alfie's dad was admitted to the hospital more than two and a half hours after the attack. He was treated for severe wounds to his arms and legs, and a blood transfusion was needed.

When at last Alfie was allowed to see his dad, he was upset to learn that he had lost part of the use of one hand.

But his dad reassured him. 'It's thanks to you that I've survived, Alfie. I'm really proud of what you did. It was very brave.'

Alfie was just glad that his dad was going to be alright after all that had happened.

A Father's Pride

January 1985

Alfred Collins, nine years old, of Marlborough, Queensland, is to receive three national bravery awards from the Royal Humane Society of Australasia. He will receive the highest honour of the Clarke Gold Medal, and also the Star of Courage and the Rupert Wilks Trophy for courage shown by a child under 13 years at the time of the brave incident.

On 26 September last year, Alfie was helping his father out on the family farm. The previous day, Alfie's father (also Alfred Collins) had noticed a large, black boar rooting up soil. While they were hunting for it, the boar took them by surprise and knocked Alfie's father to the ground, attacking him savagely.

Alfie went to his father's aid, armed only with a branch. Then he helped his badly wounded father through thick scrub back to the truck and drove him home, where his mother administered first aid.

His father was rushed to Rockhampton Hospital and admitted to the emergency department with severe wounds to his arms and legs.

Alfie will need to wait until next year to receive his awards in the nation's capital, but he says he doesn't mind. After all, they will be presented by the Queen, and he will be able to shake hands with her.

Bravery Awards

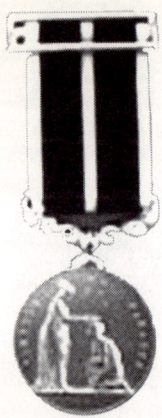

The Royal Humane Society of Australasia is one of several organisations that makes awards, commemorating acts of bravery, to those who risk their own lives in saving, or attempting to save, the lives of others.

The Clarke Gold Medal is the highest award of the Society. It is for the most outstanding case of bravery considered during the year in Australia. Very few have ever been awarded.

The Rupert Wilks Trophy is only awarded to a child under the age of 13 at the time of a brave act or rescue.

Only two people have ever been awarded both the Clarke Gold Medal and the Rupert Wilks Trophy. One of those award winners was nine-year-old Alfred Collins from Queensland, Australia.

Alfie's Award

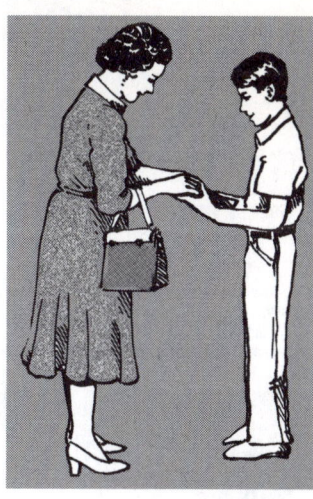

TRUE STORIES OF BRAVERY & COURAGE

BRAVE KIDS

Alfred Collins received three bravery awards for the courage he showed in rescuing his father from a near-fatal wild boar attack. The Queen presented the awards to him in 1986.

Not all acts of bravery receive awards. But when they do, they can serve as a reminder to all of us of how we rely on each other.

In this case, we are also reminded that children can do brave things too.

NEW FROM **bluecatbooks**

Inspirational
Easy-to-read
Educational

PO Box 3006
Eltham Vic 3095
Australia
+61 (03) 9439 3070

An exciting new series of amazing stories about ordinary children who displayed extraordinary bravery to save someone else's life.

FACTION: The best of both reading worlds . . . A gripping story PLUS heaps of fascinating facts set out to attract young readers.

(Crocodile Attack) . . . 'Highly recommended for building confidence in new and reluctant readers.'
. . . 'I am looking forward to seeing the next ones in the series.'
Lucinda Dodds Magpies VOLUME 19, ISSUE No 2, MAY 2004

Crocodile Attack
Peta saves her friend from the jaws of a large crocodile.

OUT February 2004
ISBN 0-9578422-4-4.

Rogue Animals
Alfie fights off a wild boar savaging his dad.

OUT July 2004
ISBN 0-9578422-7-9.

Surf Rescue
Melissa helps rescue three friends on a raft at sea.

OUT July 2004
ISBN 0-9578422-5-2.

Shark Alert
John rescues a friend from a shark attack.
ISBN 0-9578422-8 -7.

TRUE STORIES OF BRAVERY & COURAGE

www.bluecatbooks.com.au